The Singing Group Trip

By Carmel Reilly

Lou went on a trip with her singing group.

They went to sing for other kids.

Lou

Lou and the group had to fly in a plane.

They were on the plane for a long time, but Lou loves to fly.

When the group got there, they were very hungry.

They went to a souk.

A souk is a big group of shops.

the shops at the souk

A souk has lots of yummy
things to eat.

You can get meat, buns
and hot soup.

Lou **loved** the soup.

It had meat and beans in it.

The group looked at lots of things in the souk.

Lou looked at lots of bags and hats.

But then the group got lost!

A kind man showed them
the right route.

The next day, Lou's group went to a school.

Lou and her group sang for the kids.

And some kids sang songs
for Lou and her group.

Then they all had a party
with lots of things to eat
and drink.

Lou wanted more of that soup!

The next day, Lou's group
went for a fun ride
on the sand.

Then the group got
on the plane again
and went home.

Lou had a great time!

CHECKING FOR MEANING

1. Why did Lou's singing group go on a trip? *(Literal)*

2. What can you buy to eat at a souk? *(Literal)*

3. Why do you think Lou had a great time on the trip? *(Inferential)*

EXTENDING VOCABULARY

souk	What is another name for a *souk*? E.g. market. How do people move around at a souk?
soup	What is *soup*? What words do you know that can describe soup? E.g. tasty, spicy, creamy. What ingredients are used to make soup?
route	What is a *route*? What are other words that have a similar meaning? E.g. way, road, path, track.

MOVING BEYOND THE TEXT

1. Are you in a singing group at school? What songs do you sing? Why do you like singing with other people?

2. Have you been to a market? What did you see there? Did you buy anything at the market?

3. What is your favourite type of soup? Who makes this soup? What do they put in it to make it so tasty?

4. Talk about the children going on a camel ride. Where were they? Why? How do you think they got up on the camels? What do the camels do to help people get up on them?

SPEED SOUNDS

group

Lou

souk

to

route

Lou's

soup